J. S. BACH

18 SHORT PRELUDES FOR THE KEYBOARD
(12 SHORT PRELUDES AND 6 SHORT PRELUDES)

EDITED BY WILLARD A. PALMER

ORIGIN

The following account is from the first biography of J. S. Bach, written by Johann Nikolaus Forkel (1749–1817). "The first thing he did was to teach his students his particular manner of touching the instrument . . . For this purpose he made them practice, for months on end, nothing but isolated exercises for all the fingers of both hands, with constant regard to this clear and clean touch . . . But if he found that anyone, after some months of practice, began to lose patience, he was so obliging as to write appropriate little pieces in which those exercises were combined together. Of this kind are the *Sechs Kleine Praeludien* and even the fifteen *Inventionen.* He wrote these down during the hours of teaching, and in so doing attended to the momentary need of the student. But afterwards he transformed them into beautiful, expressive little works of art."

The *12 Kleine Praeludien* were probably composed under circumstances similar to those related above. Seven of these selections are found in the *Clavier-Büchlein vor Wilhelm Friedemann Bach*, a book used by J. S. Bach in the musical instruction of his son, beginning when Wilhelm Friedemann was only nine years old. The remaining preludes have been preserved only in a copy from the estate of Johann Peter Kellner (1705–1772), a personal friend of J. S. Bach, and one of his most ardent disciples and admirers, to whom we are indebted for the preservation of hundreds of Bach's works.

The *Twelve Short Preludes* were first collected and published in the middle of the 19th century by F. K. Griepenkerl, who arranged them in ascending order of keys, beginning with C Major and ending with A Minor.

The *Six Short Preludes* were first published by Hoffmeister and Kühnel, edited by J. N. Forkel. The edition contained numerous errors, according to Johann Christian Kittel, one of Bach's last students. Kittel had made a very clear copy of these preludes, now preserved in the State Library in Berlin.

The following sources were used in the preparation of the present edition:

For *Twelve Short Preludes*, Nos. 1, 4, 5, 8, 9, 10, and 11, a facsimile of the autograph of the *Clavier-Büchlein vor Wilhelm Friedemann Bach*, with permission of the music library at Yale University, New Haven, Connecticut.

For *Twelve Short Preludes*, Nos. 2, 3, 6, 7, 8, and 12, a microfilm of the manuscript from the estate of Johann Peter Kellner (Bach music manuscript No. P804), with permission of the State Library in Berlin (Preussischer Kulturbesitz).

Second Edition

Cover art: A Portrait of Johann Sebastian Bach, *1746*
by Elias Gottlieb Haussmann
Museum of Leipzig, Germany
Erich Lessing/Art Resource, New York

A CD (#16790) recording of the selections in *18 Short Preludes*, performed by Kim O'Reilly, is available separately. The CD is included with item #22522

For *Six Short Preludes,* microfilms of the following manuscripts:
P885, in the hand of Johann Christian Kittel
P540, with the identification "Graf Lichnowsky, Göttingen, 1781."
P542, a manuscript from the second half of the 18th century.

These sources are the only ones mentioned in the *Bach-Werke-Verzeichnis* of Wolfgang Schmieder, 1966 edition by Breitkopf and Härtel. All were used with the kind permission of the State Library in Berlin (Preussischer Kulturbesitz).

Two additional manuscripts used in the preparation of the Bach-Gesellschaft edition should be mentioned: P672 and P563, both of later periods than the above sources.

Also consulted in the preparation of the present edition were the Bach-Gesellschaft edition, the old Steingräber edition (Bischoff), the old Peters edition, and several recent editions.

ORNAMENTATION

1. THE APPOGGIATURA

The Italian verb "appoggiare", meaning "to lean" is descriptive of the function of the appoggiatura, which is an ornamental note receiving relatively strong emphasis before resolving to the following principal note. One German word for appoggiatura is "accent."

In his *Essay on the True Art of Playing Keyboard Instruments*, C.P.E. Bach says, "Appoggiaturas are louder than the following tone." C. P. E. Bach, Quantz, Leopold Mozart and other writers of the period give the following rules:

a. The appoggiatura is played *on the beat*.

b. The appoggiatura takes half the time of the following note, except when followed by a dotted note. It then usually takes two-thirds of the value of the note.

In some cases a certain freedom may be allowed in the application of the second of these rules, to preserve the improvisatory character of the appoggiatura.

a.  may indicate: 

b.  may indicate: 

c.  may indicate: 

d.  may indicate: 

IMPORTANT!
The modern acciaccatura or "grace note" appears in many modern editions of the music of J. S. Bach. It was never used by Bach and it is always incorrect!

2. THE TURN ~

The turn in Bach's music always begins *above* the principal note.

a.  may indicate: 

b.  may indicate: 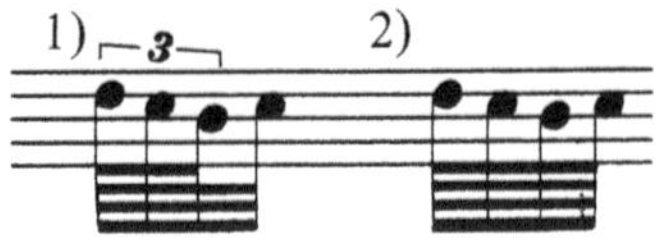

3. THE MORDENT

The word "mordent" comes from the Latin verb "mordere" (to bite). This describes the incisive quality of the mordent, which is played very quickly. It contributes brilliance to the music.

a. 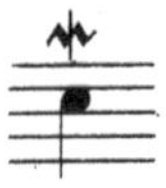 may indicate:

b.  may indicate:

Regardless of the time-values shown in the realizations, it is usually best to play mordents as quickly as possible. In extremely rapid passages, the mordent is sometimes played by striking both notes simultaneously, then immediately releasing the lower note (C.P.E. Bach, *Essay*).

4. THE TRILL

These symbols are used interchangeably to indicate a long or short trill.

All trills must begin on the upper note. This rule cannot possibly be overemphasized.

In the table of ornaments in the *Clavier-Büchlein vor Wilhelm Friedemann Bach*, Bach shows the following realization of a trill on a quarter note:

written:  played: 

The number of repercussions in the trill is determined by the tempo of the selection as well as the time value of the note upon which it occurs.

The trill may come to rest on the principal note but at times may continue for the entire value of the note. The minimum number of notes in a trill is four.

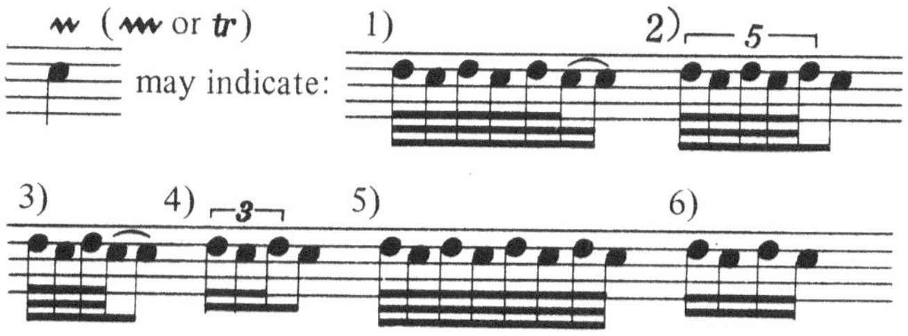

Trills on longer or shorter notes may consume the entire time value of the note or may stop on the principal note on any beat or fraction of a beat.

5. THE TRILL WITH TERMINATION

The termination consists of two notes connected to the trill, at the same speed as the trill.

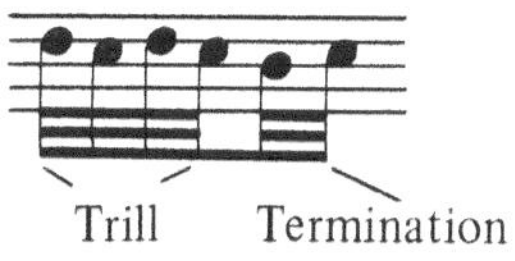

The termination may be indicated by a sign added to the trill symbol (or),or it may be written out in notes following the trill, as it is in *Prelude No. 11* on page 27, measure 30.

As the preceding example shows, the number of repercussions is optional and depends on the tempo of the selection as well as the skill and taste of the player. The values of the notes in the termination may be changed to agree with the notes of the trill.

According to the instructions of C.P.E. Bach, a termination may often be played, even when it is not indicated in the music. *Most long trills are more effective with terminations.* Short or long trills followed by the note one half-step or whole step above the principal note are usually effective with terminations.

6. THE TRILL WITH PREFIX FROM BELOW

This is sometimes called the ASCENDING TRILL.

C. P. E. Bach and D. G. Türk agree that this ornament may be written:

The prefix consists of two notes; the trill requires a minimum of four notes:

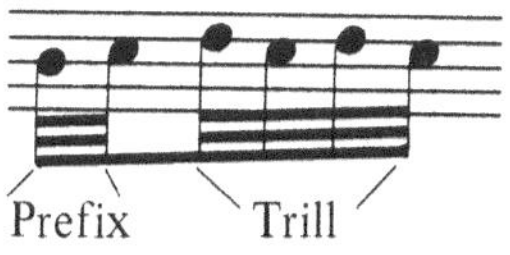

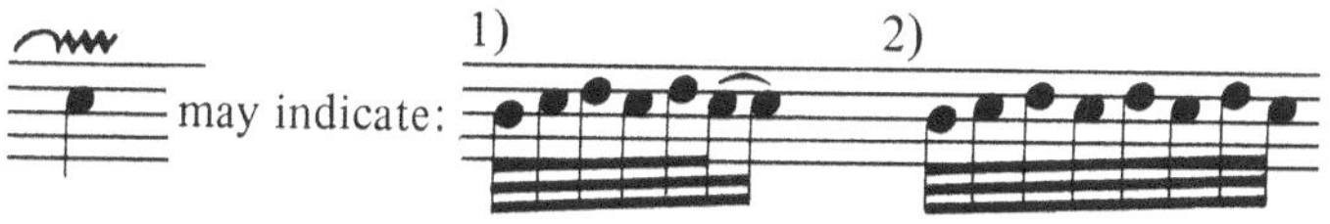

THE TRILL WITH PREFIX FROM BELOW is usually used with termination, in which case the symbol is generally used, as it is in *Prelude No. 1*, page 6, measure 3.

7. THE TRILL WITH PREFIX FROM ABOVE

This is sometimes called the DESCENDING TRILL.

The prefix from above consists of four notes and is similar to the turn; the trill requires a minimum of four notes:

THE TRILL WITH PREFIX FROM ABOVE, like the ASCENDING TRILL, usually has a termination. The symbol ⌣𝆗 is generally used, as it is in *Prelude No. 1*, page 6, measure 4.

written: played:

If the ornament is further simplified, it becomes, in effect, the same as two consecutive TURNS, and the *TRILL* does *not* have a sufficient number of repercussions:

8. THE PRALLTRILLER

The pralltriller may occur only in a descending second. The note that is ornamented with the trill must be preceded by the note one diatonic step higher. The pralltriller is played as rapidly as possible. It contains only four notes, the first of which is tied to the preceding note. The tie is indicated by a slur between the trilled note and the preceding one.

C. P. E. Bach, *Essay*:

written: played:

In these preludes, the only trills meeting the requirements of PRALLTRILLERS (that is, preceded by the upper second, which is joined to the trilled note by a slur) are found in *Prelude No. 6* of the *Six Short Preludes*. The first of these, on page 45, measure 11, is as follows:

written: played:

or: or: or:

9. THE TRILLED TURN

This ornament is illustrated in C. P. E. Bach's *Essay* as follows:

written: played:

C. P. E. Bach says it may occur with or without the preceding appoggiatura, and that it is "like a short trill with a termination." The following realizations are also acceptable:

For an example of the TRILLED TURN, refer to *Prelude No. 1* of the *Six Short Preludes*, on page 30, measure 4.

THE SIMPLIFICATION OR OMISSION OF ORNAMENTS

It is certainly acceptable to omit some of the more difficult ornaments if they are beyond the student's technical ability. In the *Clavier-Büchlein vor Wilhelm Friedemann Bach* there is evidence that J. S. Bach himself allowed his young son to omit some ornaments in the left hand part which he undoubtedly would have played himself, but being aware of his son's limitations at the time, he preferred to have the pieces played in a simplified form rather than to eliminate them entirely.

One word of caution is in order concerning the simplification of ornaments. The short trill should *never* be replaced by a so-called "upper mordent" (3). In substituting the "inverted" or "upper" mordent for a trill, one loses almost completely the dissonant function of the baroque trill, which was similar to that of the appoggiatura. In Carl Philipp Emanuel Bach's *Essay on the True Art of Playing Keyboard Instruments* he makes the following recommendation: "In very rapid tempos the effect of a trill can be achieved through the use of an appoggiatura." To illustrate this, he gives the following example:

written: simplification:

The student should be reminded that the three symbols 𝆗, 𝆗𝆗, and *tr* were used synonymously by Bach.

THE ADDITION OF ORNAMENTS

During the baroque period, few composers indicated all the ornaments they expected to be played. J. S. Bach often omitted the more obvious ones. An example of this appears on page 8. Since mordents were used in the left hand part of measure 9, mordents may be added to the same notes when they occur in measures 10 and 11.

Cadences such as the following ones should always be embellished with trills:

(a) implies: (b) implies:

In (a), the trill sounds best with a termination, because it is followed by the note a diatonic step higher.

In (b), the value of the dot may be lengthened and the eighth note played as a sixteenth. Dotted rhythms were often sharpened in this manner.

In the performance of repeated sections of pieces, ornaments were often added or varied the second time. Igor Kipnis is a master of this technique, and his recorded clavichord performance of the *12 Short Preludes* on Epic Stereo #BC 1332 deserves the attention of anyone interested in this music.

TEMPO AND DYNAMICS

There are no tempo indications and only one dynamic indication in the manuscripts of the *18 Short Preludes.*

The dynamics and tempo indications in light print have been added by the editor and may be observed according to the discretion of the teacher or student.

PHRASING AND ARTICULATION

In his biography of J. S. Bach, Forkel describes the touch Bach cultivated in his students as being such that "the tones are neither disjoined from each other nor blended together." To this he adds, "the touch is, therefore, as C. Ph. Emanuel Bach says, neither too long nor too short, but just what it ought to be." He mentioned that Bach played with curved fingers, with the tips perpendicular to the keys, and with a very quiet hand and arm. The result, he said, was "the highest degree of clearness in the expression of individual notes."

In the present edition, the slurs in lighter print were added by the editor. They should serve more to define musical ideas than to prescribe any certain degree of legato within each phrase. It is clear that Bach expected the notes to be played cleanly and well articulated at all times.

ACKNOWLEDGMENTS

I would like to express my thanks to Irving Chasnov and Morton Manus of Alfred Music Company for the meticulous care with which they helped me to prepare this edition. I also wish to thank Judith Simon Linder for her valuable assistance in the research necessary for the realization of this edition, and for her help in preparing the manuscript.

TWELVE SHORT PRELUDES

Prelude No. 1

J. S. Bach

Molto moderato M.M. ♩=60-66 **(or slower)**

ⓐ If possible, the ornament should be played: 

This is more compatible with the correct realization of the ornament discussed in footnote ⓑ.

ⓑ The realization shown is a simplification.
The following is more correct: 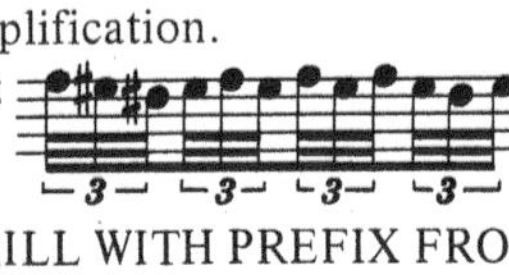

See the discussion of THE TRILL WITH PREFIX FROM ABOVE, on page 4.

ⓒ Better: 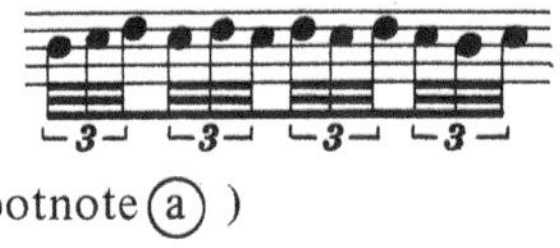

(See footnote ⓐ)

ⓓ In the autograph, as in our text, there are no ties joining the lower G's here or in measures 14 - 15. C.P.E. Bach states in his *Essay*, "The performer may break a long tied note by restriking the key."

Prelude No. 2

ⓐ Avoid making breaks between the slurs conspicuous.

ⓑ The Kellner manuscript has B instead of G. We accept the version of the Bach-Gesellschaft.

ⓒ The Kellner manuscript has G instead of E.

ⓓ The trill at the cadence is appropriate. It does not appear in the manuscript. See the discussion on THE ADDITION OF ORNAMENTS, p. 5.

Prelude No. 3

The title, in the Kellner manuscript, is *Praelude in C moll pour la Lute di J. S. Bach* (Prelude in C Minor for the lute, by J. S. Bach).

(a) Several editions have D instead of C. The C is correct.

28
en-
do
p
31
34
poco cresc-
-en
37
do
dim.
40
p
poco rit.
mf

Prelude No. 4

ⓐ The D is clear in the *Clavier-Büchlein*. The Bach-Gesellschaft edition omits this D, stating it is believed to be an error, probably because it gives the effect of consecutive octaves with the bass (A-D).

ⓑ In a copy of the *Clavier-Büchlein* in the Amalien-Bibliothek (not an autograph), a fermata appears over the 1st eighth note in the measure. This may indicate an optional ending, or perhaps a pause before continuing. *Poco ritardando* at the deceptive cadence in measure 14 is appropriate and might logically lead to such a fermata, with *a tempo* at the return of the principal theme in measure 15. The fermata does not appear in the original autograph of the *Clavier-Büchlein*.

Prelude No. 5

Con moto M.M. ♩ = 120 – 132

ⓐ The slurs in dark print are from the autograph. It is impossible, however, to determine exactly which notes they encompass.

16
20
24
28
32

ⓑ Bach originally wrote only  The C and A were apparently added later, in smaller notes, by Bach himself.

The copy in the Amalien-Bibliothek has 

Prelude No. 6

Andante moderato M.M. ♩ = 48–54

ⓐ In the Kellner manuscript, the A is a half note.

Prelude No. 7

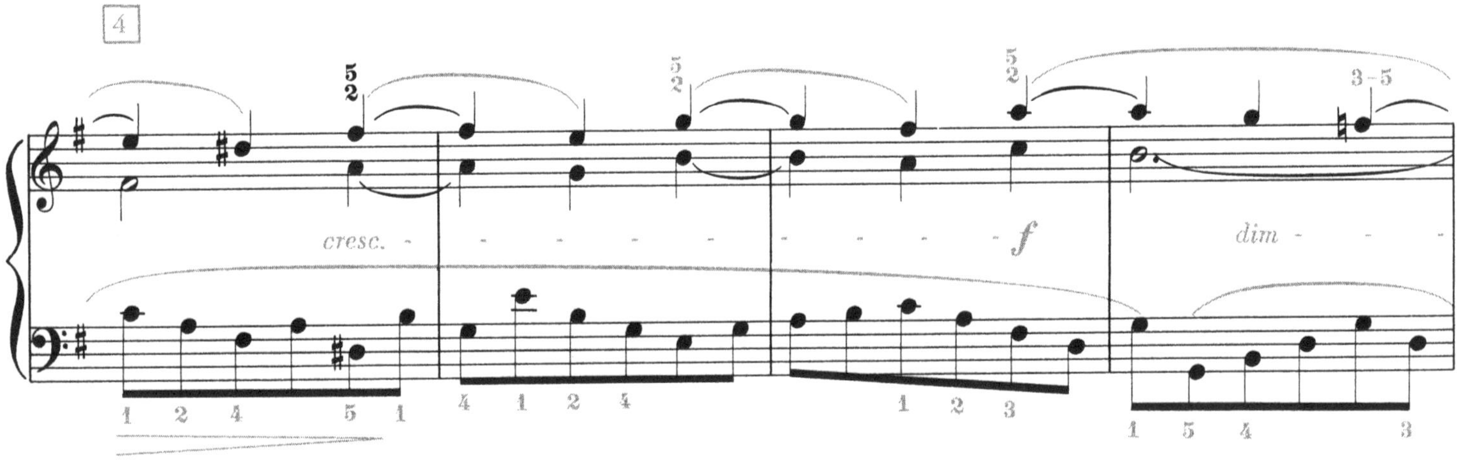

ⓐ The E's are not tied, as most editions show.

ⓑ Kellner has A instead of G.

ⓒ The manuscript clearly shows a mordent here rather than a trill. Because the trill is so much more effective at the cadence than the mordent, we have included it in our realizations. The Bach-Gesellschaft and Bischoff editions show a trill. The value of the dot may be lengthened, and the last note of the measure (G) played as a sixteenth note.

ⓓ The triplet against two eighths is surprising, since this combination of rhythms is unusual in music of this period. The Bischoff and Bach-Gesellschaft editions show the second of the two eighths in the lower voices positioned as if they should be played with the last note of the triplet, as was sometimes the practice in the baroque period. The use of this device for one beat of the entire selection is not very satisfying. It is possible that this is a rare case of the deliberate use of "two against three" rhythm.

ⓔ The trill is missing in the manuscript but is appropriate at the cadence. The value of the dot may be lengthened, and the last note of the measure (E) played as a sixteenth note.

Prelude No. 8

ⓐ Bischoff has F instead of G. According to the Bach-Gesellschaft, this is a "musically good conjecture, but conflicting with all manuscripts."

ⓑ Most editors show the chord in eighth notes. This may be traced to the Kellner manuscript. The *Clavier-Büchlein* has the notes of the chord in three separate voices, all clearly quarter notes.

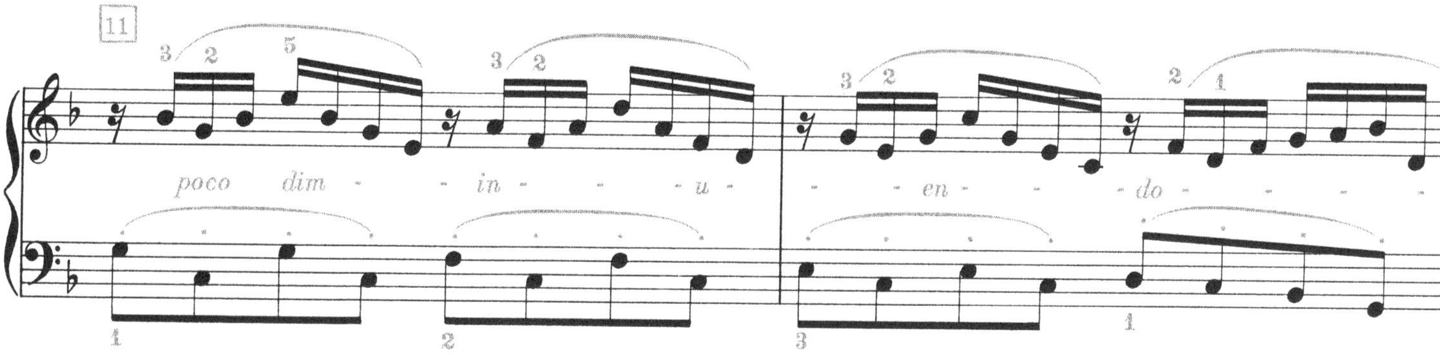

Ⓒ  in most editions. Our text agrees with the *Clavier-Büchlein* as well as the Kellner manuscript.

Prelude No. 9

Con moto . M.M. ♩= 66–72 (♪ =132–144)

cresc.

ⓐ The cadence demands a trill, although it does not appear in the *Clavier-Büchlein*. The trill may have more repercussions, and the value of the dot may be lengthened.

ⓑ The C in light print is missing in the *Clavier-Büchlein* but is probably correct. It appears in the Bach-Gesellschaft edition.

Prelude No. 10

This selection appears in the *Clavier-Büchlein* in the handwriting of Wilhelm Friedemann Bach. At the beginning is written "Menuet trio di J. S. Bach." It was composed not as a prelude but as a trio for the menuet of Stölzel's *Partita*. Because it was included in the original collection of *12 Kleine Praeludien*, it is now best known as a prelude.

Prelude No. 11

Andante sostenuto M.M. ♩ = 80–88

This prelude appears in the *Clavier-Büchlein vor Wilhelm Friedemann Bach* in the hand of J. S. Bach. The fingering in dark print is Bach's own and is one of only three known examples of Bach's fingering.

ⓐ The A probably should be held for the remainder of the measure.

29
meno f
32
f
35
39
f

Prelude No. 12

ⓐ The smaller staff is a variant added by Bischoff in an effort to improve the counterpoint. The text in dark print is in agreement with the Kellner manuscript, which is the only known source for this prelude.

ⓑ A sharp appears before the G in the manuscript, probably an error.

ⓒ The notes in light print are taken from the Bach-Gesellschaft edition. In the manuscript, the left hand part of the previous measure was copied again here through error.

ⓓ The trill does not appear in the manuscript but is appropriate at the cadence. It may be played with a termination: 

SIX SHORT PRELUDES

Prelude No. 1

J. S. Bach

Molto moderato M.M. ♩ = 54 – 66

ⓐ The forte indication appears in P540, P542 and the Kittel manuscript (P885).

ⓑ The trill appears only in the Kittel manuscript. P540 and P542 have no ornament here. P528 and P672 have a G appoggiatura instead of the trill.

ⓒ All the important manuscripts clearly indicate the trilled turn. Only P540 has the C appoggiatura. The ornament may be simplified as follows:  See the discussion on the TRILLED TURN on page 4.

ⓓ Avoid a conspicuous break between the slurs.

ⓔ Kittel has G instead of A. The other manuscripts have A.

ⓕ The mordents in lighter print are from the Kittel manuscript.

ⓖ The Kittel manuscript has a fermata over the last note.

Prelude No. 2

ⓐ The Kittel manuscript has a trill above the note following the appoggiatura, and similarly in measure 4.

ⓑ The appoggiatura may be added; it does not appear in any of the manuscripts.

Prelude No. 3

ⓐ The trill is from the Kittel manuscript (P885). P540 has a mordent. The Lichnowsky manuscript (P542) has no ornament and no tie. P528 has ⁓. The trill demands a termination whether indicated or not.

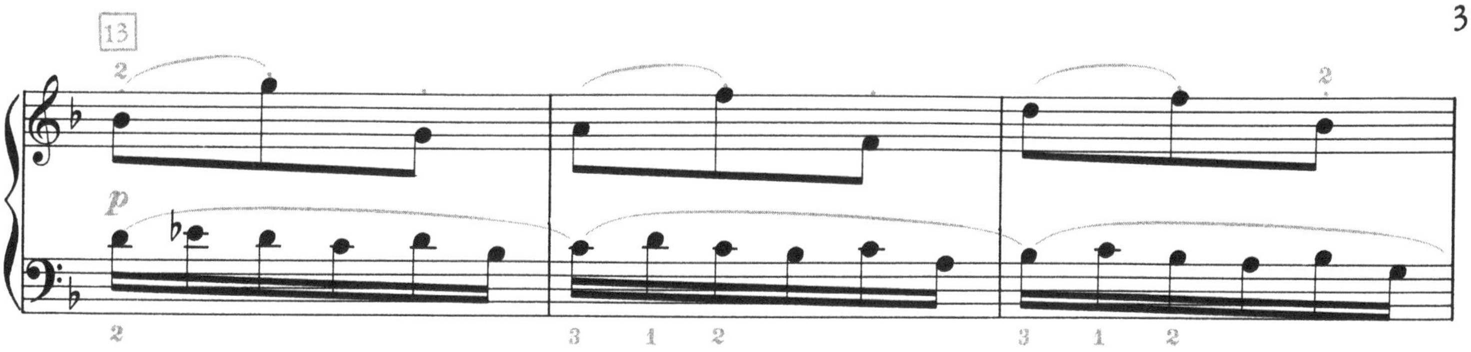

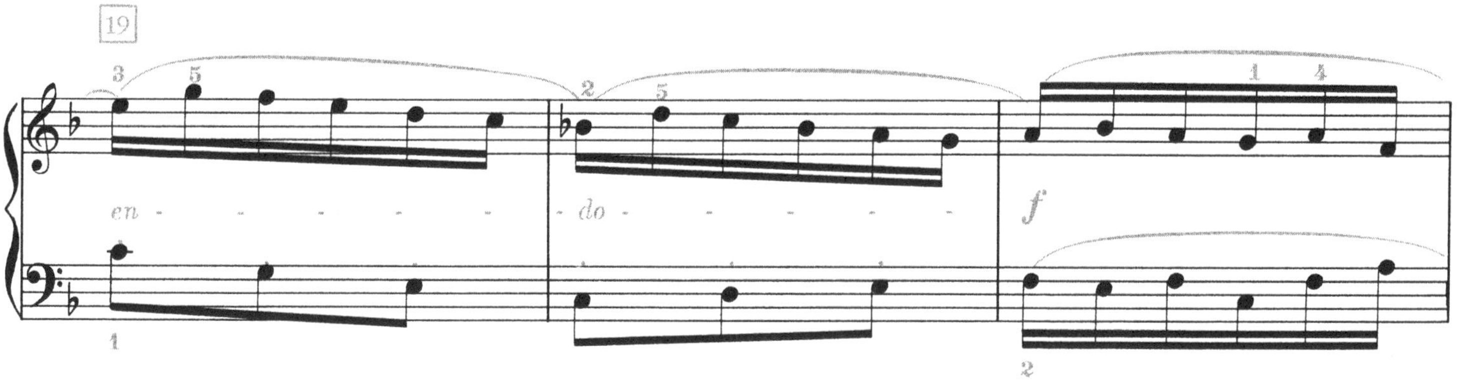

ⓑ This measure is given as it appears in P540. In the Kittel and Lichnowsky manuscripts it appears: 

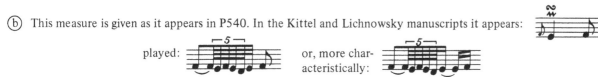

played:  or, more characteristically: 

The version we have selected is not only simpler but, in the editor's opinion, more musical. The trill may be played with additional repercussions.

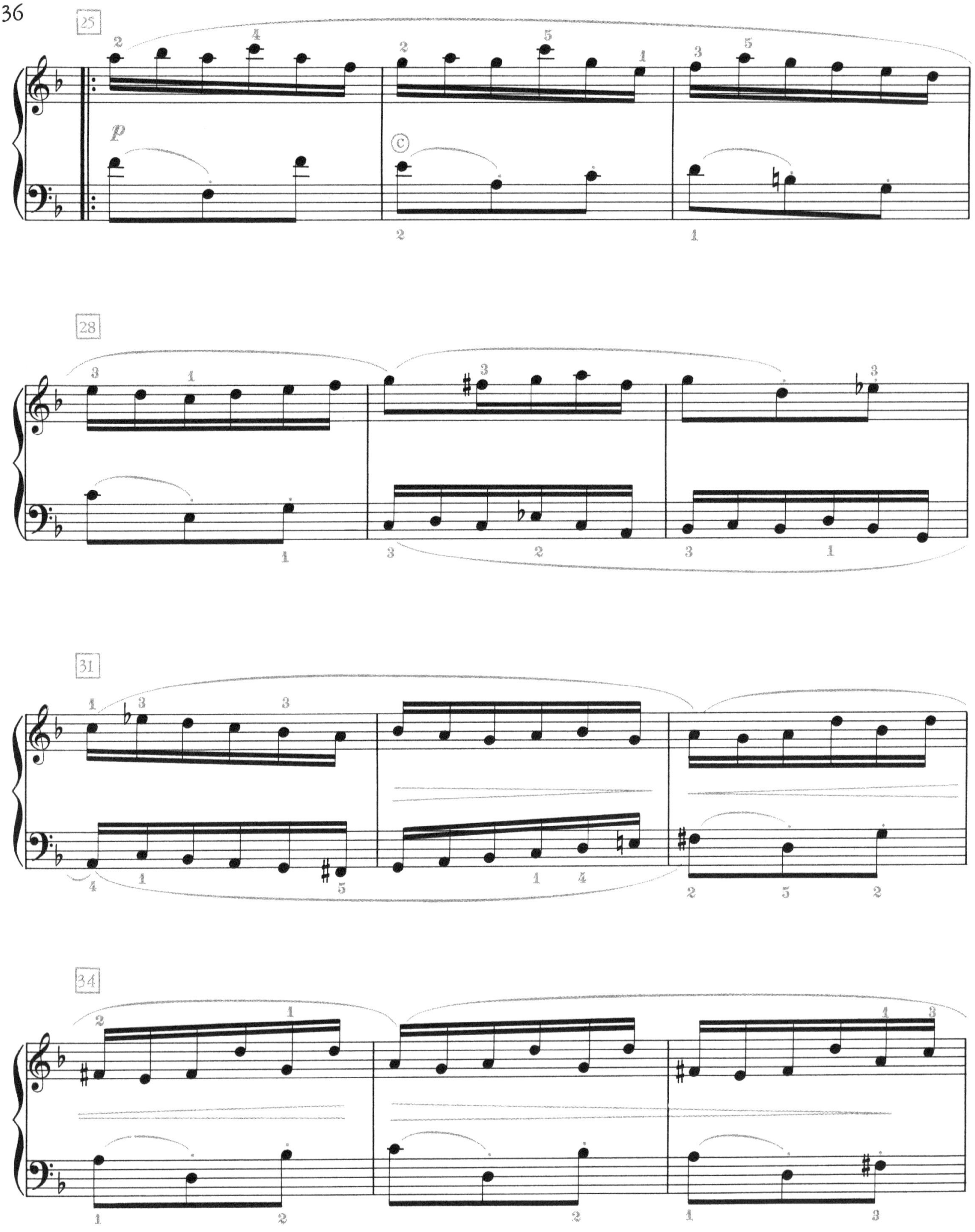

ⓒ The Bischoff edition has  This certainly sounds more correct. Our text is in agreement, however, with all the manuscripts and with the Bach-Gesellschaft edition.

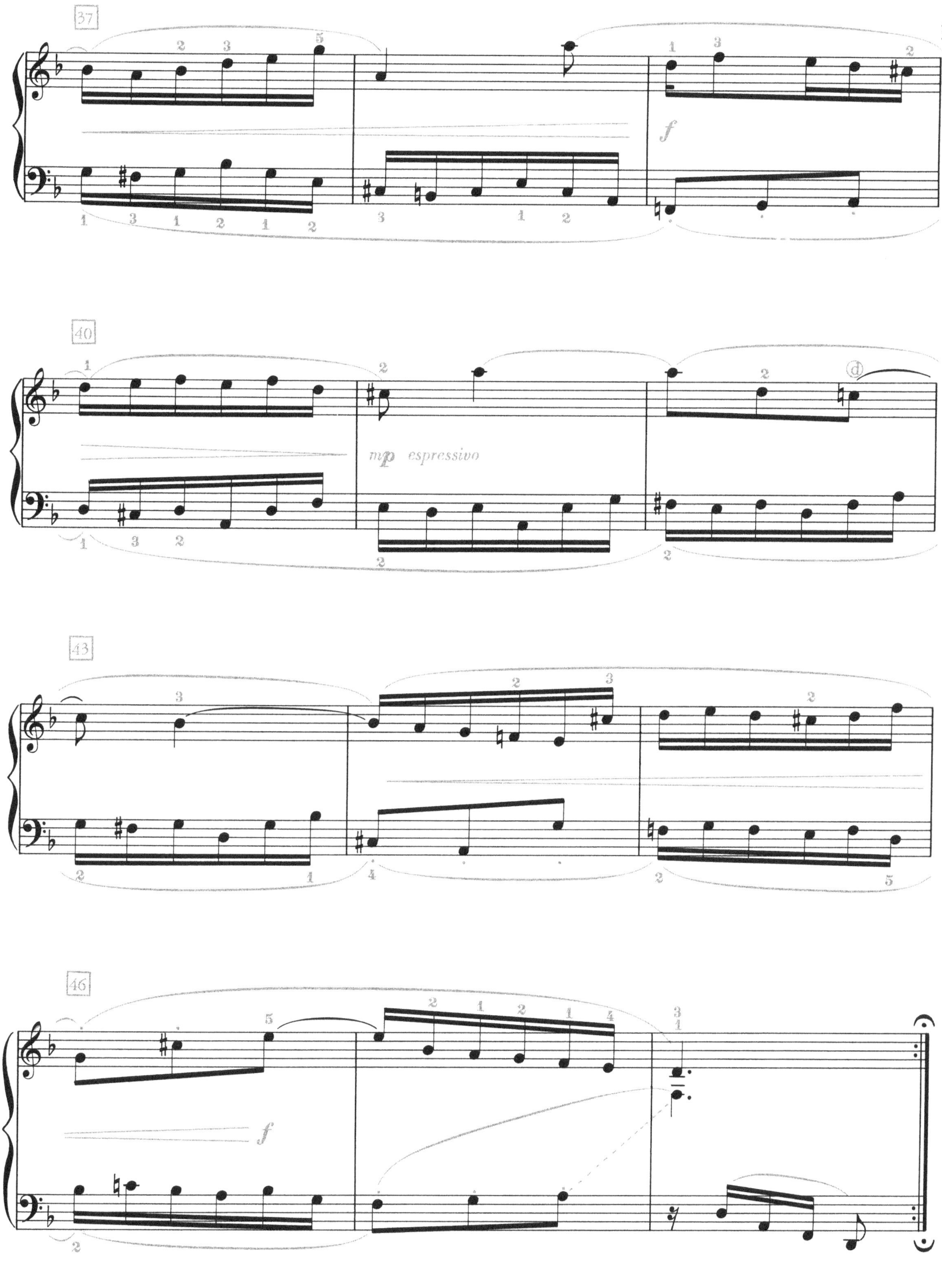

ⓓ The tie is missing in P542.

Prelude No. 4

The eighth notes in the left hand accompaniment were probably played *non legato* on the harpsichord, to bring the upper voices into greater prominence. On the piano, they may be played *legato* or *non legato*, at the discretion of the individual.

ⓐ The trill is in the Kittel manuscript. If it is observed, it should probably be applied also to the 1st treble note of the next 3 measures, as indicated by the ornaments in light print.

ⓑ The slurs in dark print are from the Kittel manuscript.

ⓒ The smaller slurs are suggested by the stem directions in the three manuscripts. They may be played so as to give the impression of two separate voices but need not be separated by perceptible breaks between slurs.

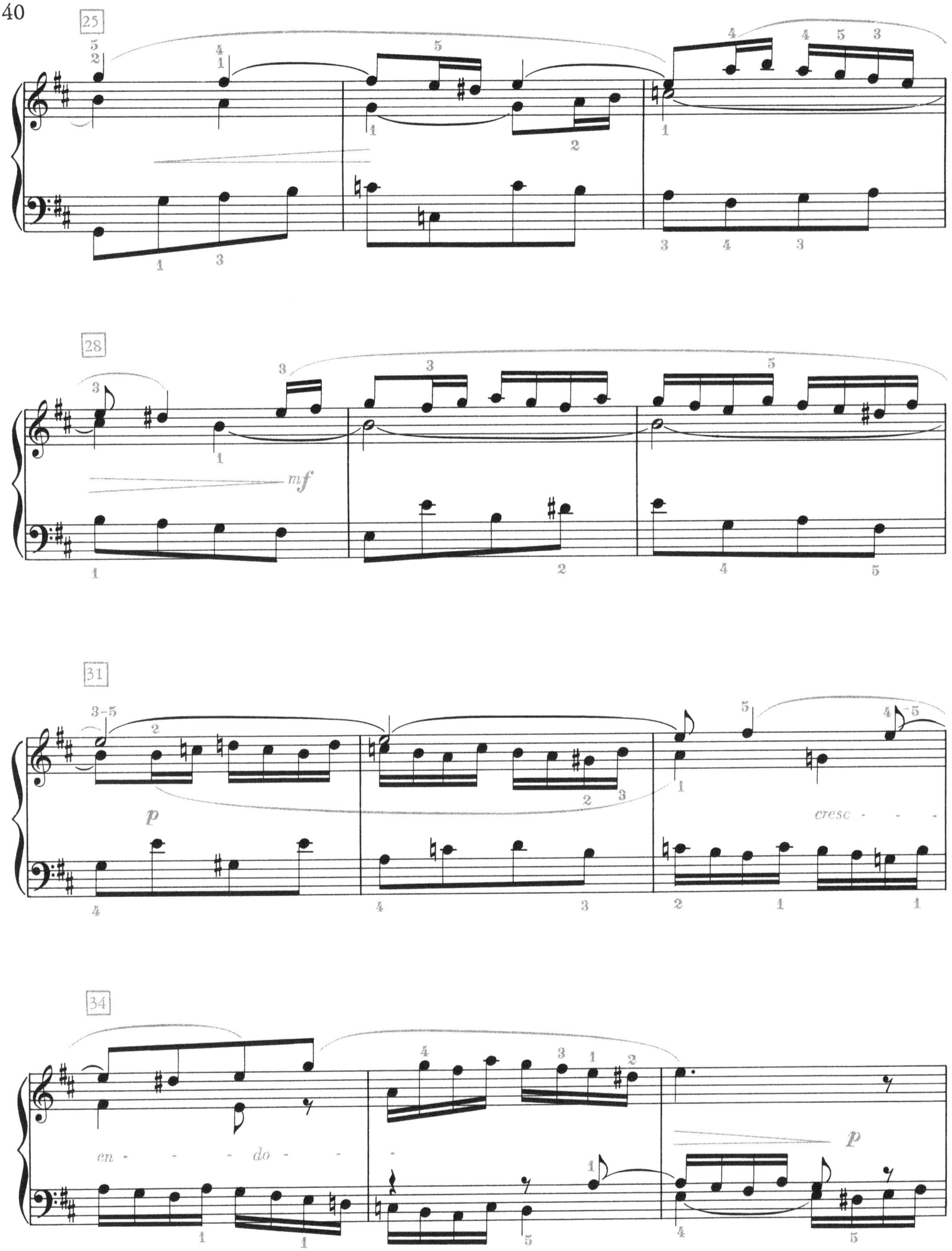
25
28
mf
31
p
cresc
34
en
do
p

(d) See footnote (c), on page 39.

(e) The tie is missing in P542.

Prelude No. 5

ⓐ The trill is missing in P542 and in the Kittel manuscript.

ⓑ The trill at the cadence may be played with a suffix:  or with an anticipation: 

This trill is difficult at the indicated tempo. It may be played the 2nd time only, with a ritardando in the final measure.

Prelude No. 6

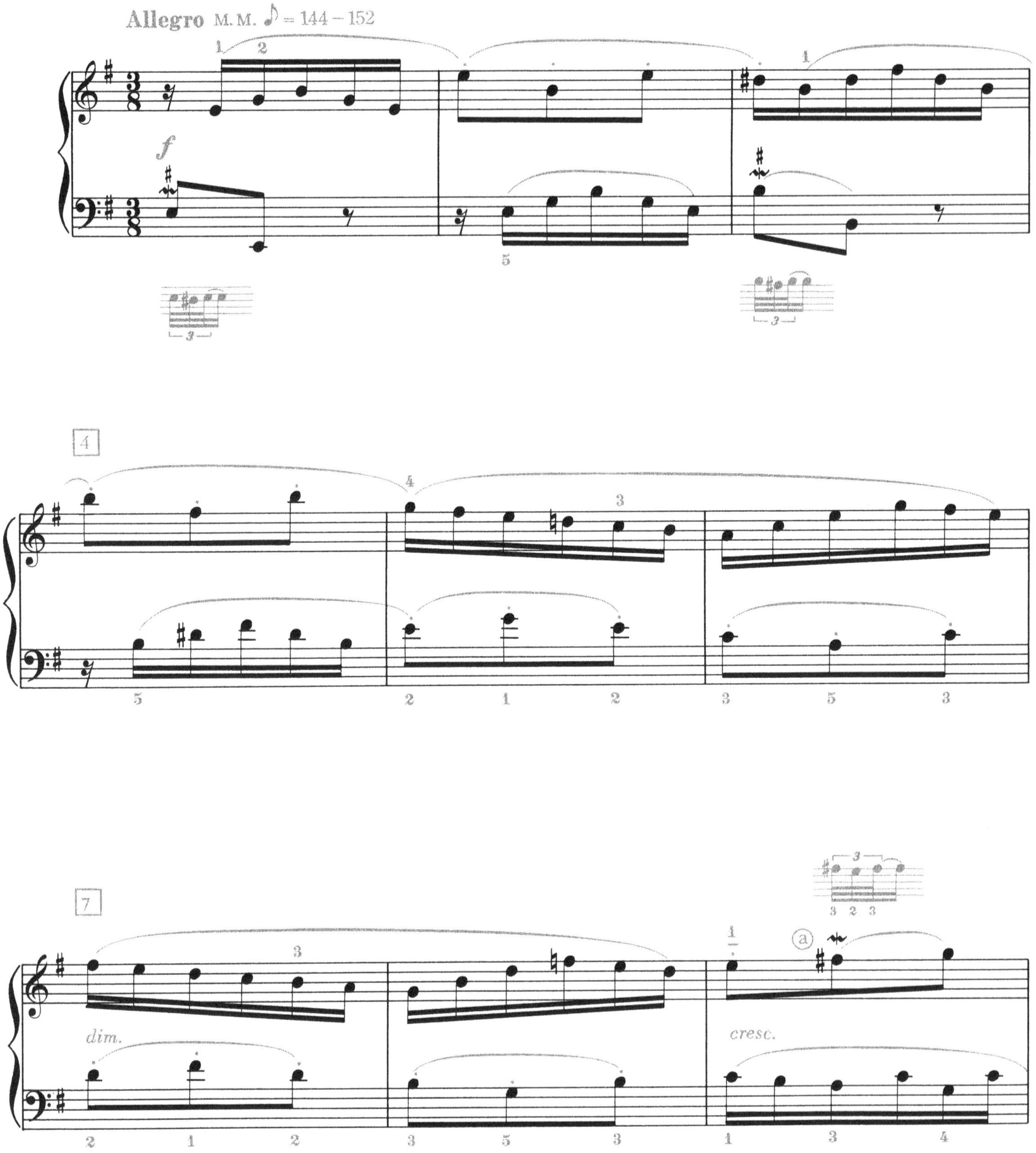

ⓐ The Kittel manuscript shows [ornament], which implies additional repercussions.
The other manuscripts have [ornament].

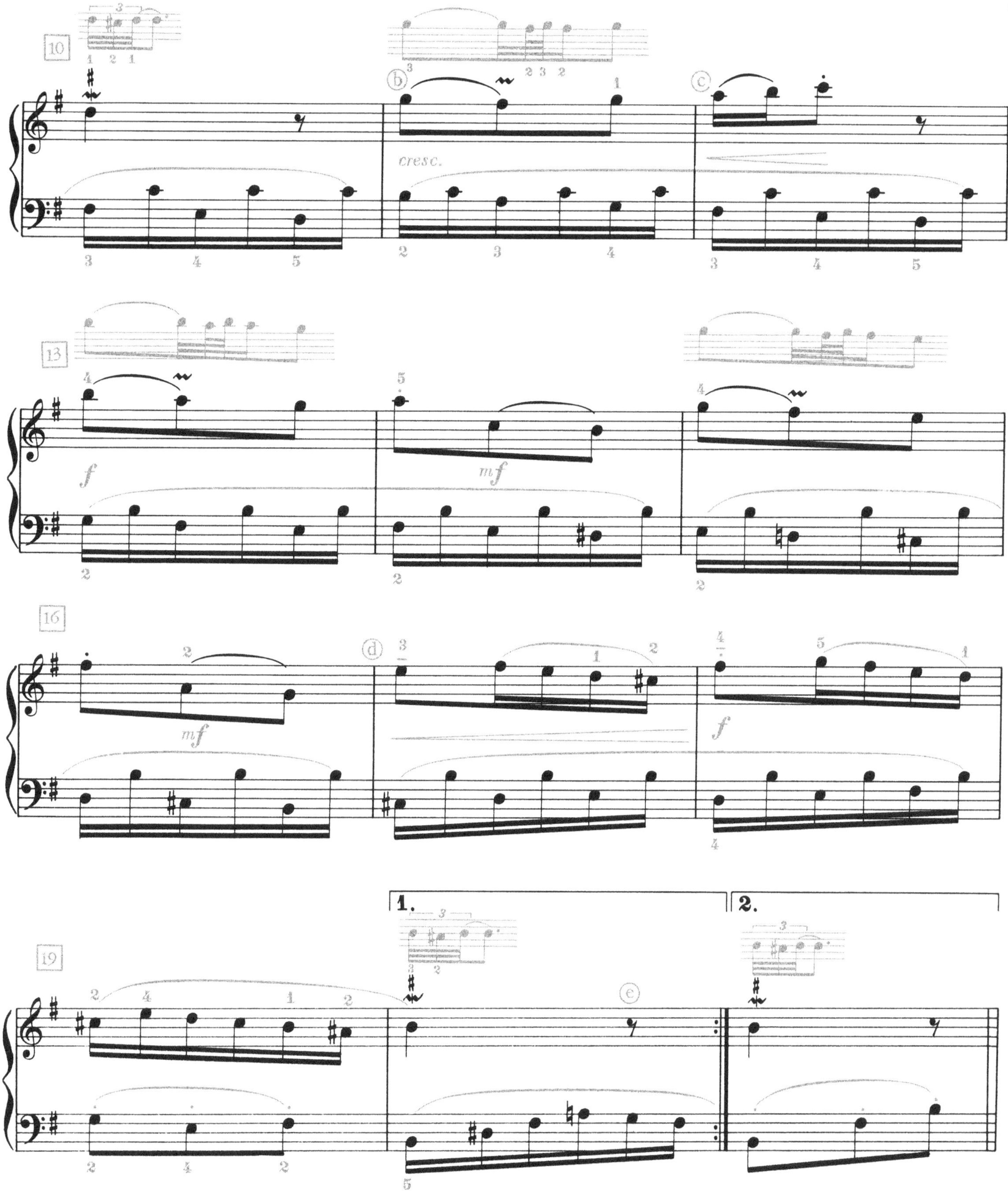

ⓑ The slur in dark print here and in measures 13, 15, 23, 25, 42 and 44 are from P540. These slurs indicate that the ornament is performed as a pralltriller, as shown in our realizations. See page 4.

Short trills may be played instead of the pralltrillers, if preferred. This would be in agreement with the Kittel manuscript, which does not have the slurs. P542 has a mordent instead of the trill in measures 11, 13, 15, 23 and 42, but has a trill in 25 and 44 and is thus inconsistent.

ⓒ The slur and staccato here and in measures 14 and 16 are from the Kittel manuscript.

ⓓ A mordent appears over the E in P528 and P672.

ⓔ The eighth rest here and in the following measure and the eighth rests in the 1st and 2nd endings on page 47 are from the Kittel manuscript. The other manuscripts have ♩. and no rest, in each instance.

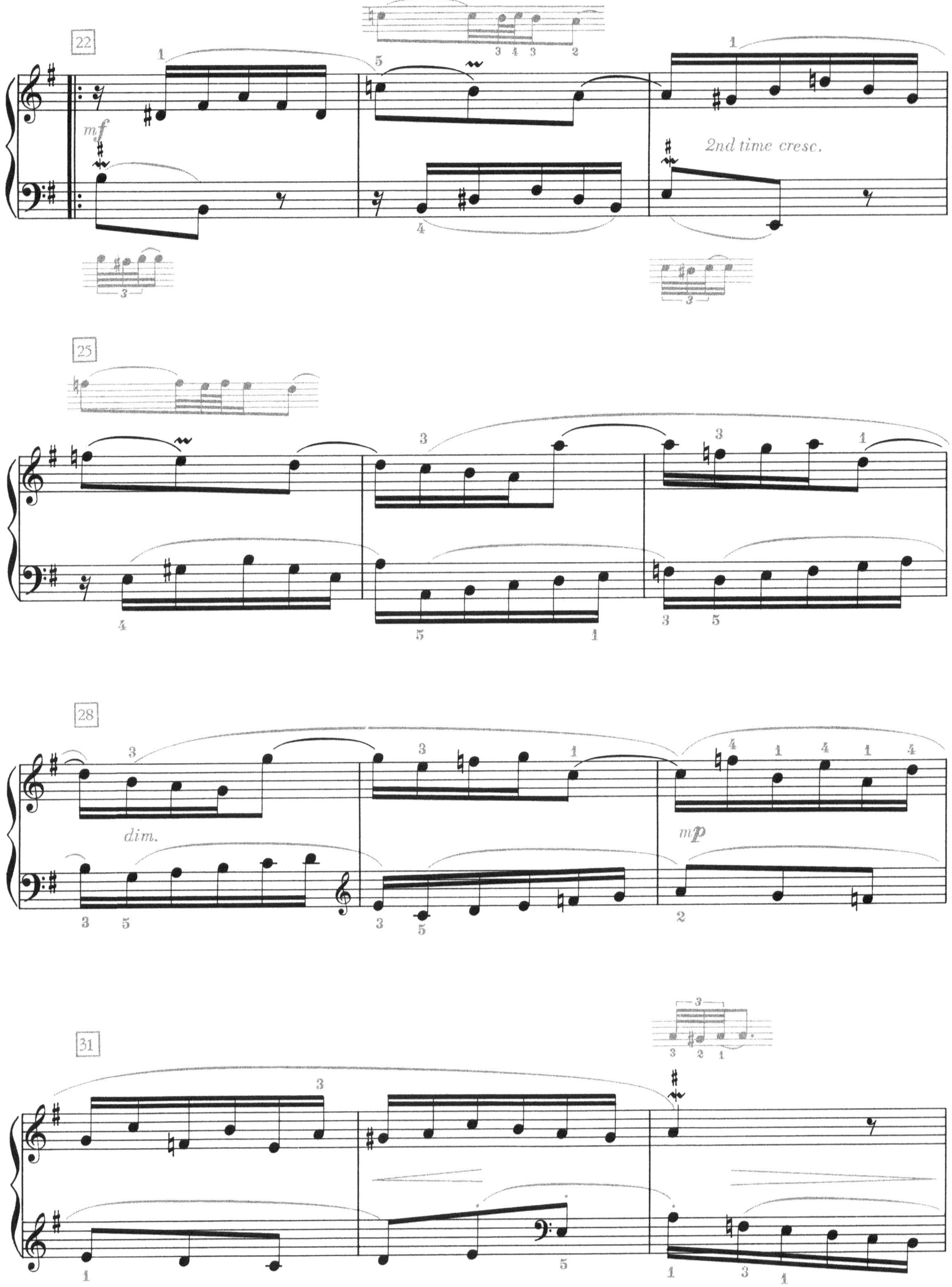
22
mf
2nd time cresc.
25
28
dim.
mp
31

34
37
cresc.
41
f
mf
44
mf
47
f
1.
2.

THEMATIC INDEX

TWELVE SHORT PRELUDES

BWV 924 Page

1.  6

BWV 939

2.  8

BWV 999

3.  9

BWV 925

4.  12

BWV 926

5.  14

BWV 940

6.  17

BWV 941 Page

7.  18

BWV 927

8.  20

BWV 928

9.  21

BWV 929

10.  24

BWV 930

11.  25

BWV 942

12.  28

SIX SHORT PRELUDES

BWV 933 Page

1.  30

BWV 934

2.  32

BWV 935

3.  34

BWV 936 Page

4.  38

BWV 937

5.  42

BWV 938

6.  44